The Most Adorable
ANIMALS
IN THE WORLD

by Tammy Gagne

CAPSTONE PRESS
a capstone imprint

First Facts are published by Capstone Press,
1710 Roe Crest Drive, North Mankato, Minnesota 56003
www.capstonepub.com

Library of Congress Cataloging-in-Publication Data
Gagne, Tammy, author.
The most adorable animals in the world / by Tammy Gagne.
pages cm.—(First facts. All about animals)
Summary: "Interesting facts, colorful photographs, and simple text introduce readers to the
world's cutest animals"—Provided by publisher.
Audience: Ages 6-9.
Audience: K to grade 3.
Includes bibliographical references and index.
ISBN 978-1-4914-2053-9 (library binding)
ISBN 978-1-4914-2239-7 (paperback)
ISBN 978-1-4914-2259-5 (ebook pdf)
1. Mammals—Juvenile literature. 2. Mammals—Miscellanea—Juvenile literature. I. Title.
QL706.2.G34 2015
599.02—dc23   2014032053

Editorial Credits
Kathryn Clay, editor; Bobbie Nuytten, designer; Jo Miller, media researcher; Kathy
McColley, production specialist

Photo Credits
iStockphotos: charmedesign, 5, 22, Craig Dingle, 19, 22; Shutterstock: Cat Downie, cover
(bottom right), Eric Gevaert, 21, 22, hjschneider, 15, 22, iravgustin, 14, Joe Ravi, cover
(middle), 7, 22, Martchan, cover (top), 1, meunierd, 13, 22, nattanan726, 11, 22, Robyn
Mackenzie, 18, sevenke, 6, Sourav and Joyeeta, 10, Tory Kallman, 17, 22, Vladimir Melnik,
cover (bottom left), 9, 22, wormig, 22 (map)

Table of Contents

Quokka

Large or small. Fluffy or feathered. Animals have physical **traits** that set them apart from one another. Some traits make animals look scary or unfriendly. Other traits are simply adorable. The quokka always appears to be smiling. Unlike many wild animals, this Australian **marsupial** is known for being extremely friendly.

trait—a feature or quality about something that makes it different from others

marsupial—a group of mammals in which the females feed and carry their young in pouches

Fact: Most quokkas are found on Rottnest Island off the southwest coast of Australia.

Red Panda

Many people are surprised by the red panda's appearance. Found in China, red pandas look more like raccoons than pandas. Their red and white coloring provides **camouflage** in the bamboo forests where they live.

camouflage—a pattern or color on an animal that helps it blend in with the things around it

Fact: Red pandas have soft fur all over their bodies. Even the soles of their feet are covered with fur.

7

Harp Seal

Adorable animals live on land and in the sea. The harp seal lives in the North Atlantic and Arctic Oceans. Baby harp seals have white fur. The thick fur coat and layer of **blubber** keep the animals warm in icy waters. The fluffy white fur is also valuable. Many harp seals are hunted each year for their prized **pelts**.

blubber—a thick layer of fat under the skin of some animals; blubber keeps animals warm

pelt—an animal's skin with the hair or fur still on it

Fact: Mother harp seals can find their babies among hundreds of others just by scent.

Fennec Fox

The fennec fox of northern Africa has huge, pointed ears. The long ears remove heat from the animal's body during hot days in the desert. A long, thick coat keeps the fox warm at night.

Fact: Fennec foxes are the smallest members of the canidae family. This group includes wolves, coyotes, and dogs.

Chinchilla

Wild chinchillas live in the Andes Mountains of South America. They have the softest fur of all **mammals**. Their fur is sometimes used to make clothing. But because of overhunting, chinchillas are now considered **endangered**.

mammal—a warm-blooded animal that breathes air; mammals have hair or fur; female mammals feed milk to their young

endangered—at risk of dying out

Fact: To clean their fur, chinchillas roll around in dust. The dust soaks up oil and dirt.

Alpaca

Like chinchillas, wild alpacas live in the mountains of South America. Some people raise these friendly, gentle animals on farms. Their fleece is used to make yarn for clothing. Many farms even allow families to visit and pet the animals.

Fact: Alpaca fleece is softer than cashmere and warmer than wool.

Bottlenose Dolphin

Bottlenose dolphins are not only cute. They are also among the smartest creatures in the world. These members of the whale family are quite social. Living in groups of two to 15, they communicate with one other through sound. Each dolphin has a unique whistle. Scientists have found that dolphins use these sounds to identify one another.

Koala

The koala is often called a koala "bear" by mistake. But this cuddly animal is actually a marsupial like the quokka. Koalas live in **eucalyptus** trees in Australia. Because they eat the trees' leaves, most koalas rarely come down to the ground. They get most of their water from the eucalyptus leaves.

eucalyptus—a fragrant evergreen tree that grows in dry climates

Fact: A koala can eat as much as 2.5 pounds (1 kilogram) of eucalyptus leaves each day.

Emperor Tamarin

The emperor tamarin appears to have a long, white moustache. This small type of monkey lives in the forests of South America. Emperor tamarins are social animals that live together in troops. Each troop has two to eight members and is led by the oldest female.

Fact: The emperor tamarin received its name from a Swiss scientist. The scientist joked that the animal looked like the former German emperor Wilhelm II. The emperor also had a long moustache.

Range Map

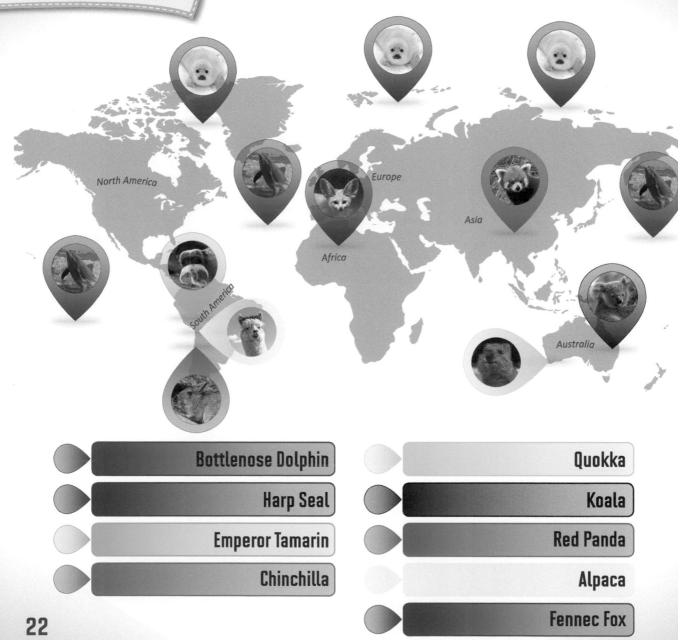

North America

Europe

Africa

Asia

South America

Australia

Bottlenose Dolphin	Quokka
Harp Seal	Koala
Emperor Tamarin	Red Panda
Chinchilla	Alpaca
	Fennec Fox

Glossary

blubber (BLUH-buhr)—a thick layer of fat under the skin of some animals; blubber keeps animals warm

camouflage (KA-muh-flahzh)—a pattern or color on an animal that helps it blend in with the things around it

endangered (in-DAYN-juhrd)—at risk of dying out

eucalyptus (yoo-kuh-LIP-tuhs)—a fragrant evergreen tree that grows in dry climates

mammal (MAM-uhl)—a warm–blooded animal that breathes air; mammals have hair or fur; female mammals feed milk to their young

marsupial (mar-SOO-pee-uhl)—a group of mammals in which the females feed and carry their young in pouches

pelt (PELT)—an animal's skin with the hair or fur still on it

trait (TRATE)—a feature or quality about something that makes it different from others

Critical Thinking Using the Common Core

1. How does a red fox blend in with its environment? (Key Ideas and Details)

2. Reread page 12 about how chinchillas are considered endangered. What can people do to protect chinchillas? (Integration of Knowledge and Ideas)

Read More

Drumlin, Sam. *Harp Seals*. Sea Friends. New York: PowerKids Press, 2013.

Hughes, Catherine D. *First Big Book of Animals*. National Geographic Little Kids. Washington, D.C.: National Geographic, 2010.

Kawa, Katie. *Baby Koalas*. Cute and Cuddly: Baby Animals. New York: Gareth Stevens Pub., 2012.

Internet Sites

FactHound offers a safe, fun way to find Internet sites related to this book. All of the sites on FactHound have been researched by our staff.

Here's all you do:
Visit *www.facthound.com*
Type in this code: 9781491420539

Super-cool stuff!

Check out projects, games and lots more at
www.capstonekids.com

Index